W9-CAZ-360

Discard

Discard

I Know That!

Seeing

Claire Llewellyn

SEA-TO-SEA
Mankato Collingwood London

This edition first published in 2006 by
Sea-to-Sea Publications
1980 Lookout Drive
North Mankato
Minnesota 56003

Copyright © Sea-to-Sea Publications 2006
Text copyright © Claire Llewellyn 2004, 2006

Printed in China

All rights reserved

Library of Congress Cataloging-in-Publication Data

Llewellyn, Claire.
  Seeing/by Claire Llewellyn
    p. cm. — (I know that!)
  Simultaneously published: Mankato, Minn.: Smart Apple Media, 2004.
  Includes index.
  ISBN 1-932889-48-5
  1. Vision—Juvenile literature. I. Title.

QP475.7.L78 2005
612.8'4—dc22

                                    2004062741

9 8 7 6 5 4 3 2

Published by arrangement with the Watts Publishing Group Ltd, London

Series advisers: Gill Matthews, nonfiction literacy consultant and Inset trainer. Editor: Rachel Cooke.
Series design: Peter Scoulding. Designer: James Marks. Photography: Ray Moller unless otherwise credited.
Acknowledgments: Harold Chapman/Topham: 11t. Corbis: 10. Chris Fairclough/Franklin Watts: 16, 18, 21r.
Michael Gore/Ecoscene: 9tr Klein/Still Pictures: 13tr. Mostyn/Eye Ubiquitous: 9b, 15t. Paul Seheult/Eye
Ubiquitous: 19. Joseph Sohm/Image Works/Topham: 14. Thanks to our models, including Vanessa Dang,
Sophie Hall, Latifah Harris, Thomas Howe, Amelia Menicou, Spencer Mulchay, and Ishar Sehgal.

Contents

We see with our eyes

Every day we use our eyes to see the world around us. Seeing is one of our senses.

▶ *We use our eyes to read a book...*

choose some fruit…

We have five senses. They are seeing, hearing, tasting, smelling, and touching.

pour a drink…

and look in the mirror.

Looking at eyes

We have two eyes on our face.

▼ *Our eyes can be brown…*

blue…

gray…

or green.

Eyes have many different parts.

Eyelid

Eyelash

Find a mirror and look at your eyes. What color are they?

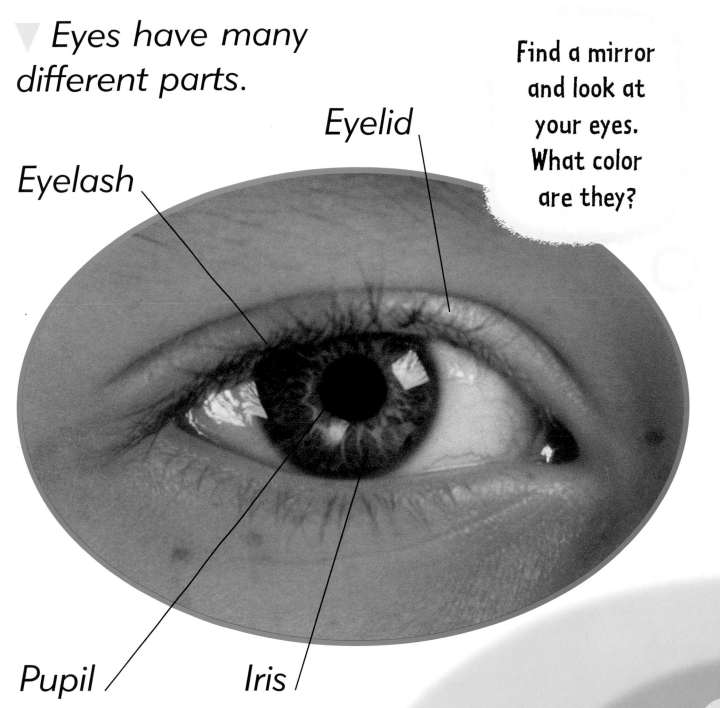

Pupil

Iris

We need light to see

We see when light enters our eyes.
When there is no light, we cannot see.

► *When we turn the light off at night, it is too dark to see.*

A flashlight gives us light to see in the dark.

An owl feeds at night. Its big eyes help it to see in the dark.

We see in color

Our eyes can see the colors in the world around us.

▶ *We see all the colors of the rainbow.*

Bees see in color, too. When they see colorful flowers, they land on them and feed.

▼ We like colorful clothes.

▲ We stop when we see a red light; we go when the light turns green.

Using our eyes

We use our eyes to see whether things are big or small.

▶ *We can see the pullover is too big!*

12

We use our eyes
to see what
is near or
far away.

A cat's eyes tell
it how far it has
to jump to land
safely.

◀ We can
see the toy is
nearer than
the chair.

Keeping safe

Our eyes help us find our way.
They keep us safe.

▲ *We can follow the signs.*

We look both ways before we cross the road.

How do your eyes help to keep you safe on your way to school?

We see *if something* is in our way.

Wearing glasses

Some people cannot see clearly. They have glasses to help them.

▶ *This girl is having her eyes tested.*

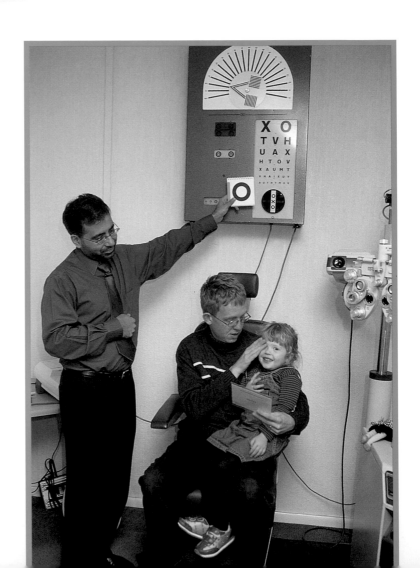

Glasses help people to see clearly.

We go to the optician's to have our eyes tested. Opticians are eye experts.

Some people wear contact lenses instead.

Some people cannot see

Blind people see very badly. Some blind people cannot see anything at all.

▶ *Some blind people have a guide dog to help them find their way.*

Blind people read letters made of dots.

When blind people read, which of their five senses are they using?

Looking after our eyes

Our eyes are very important.
We must look after them.

▶ *Always read with plenty of light...*

and wear sunglasses on a sunny day.

When we blink, our eyelids wipe our eyes. This keeps them clean.

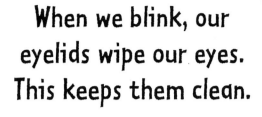

▼ Have you had an eye test? Every child should have one.

Don't look at the Sun. It can damage your eyes.

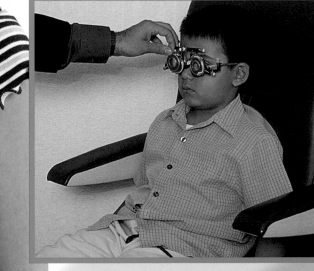

I know that...

1 We use our eyes to see.

2 Seeing is one of our senses.

3 Our eyes can be brown, blue, gray, or green.

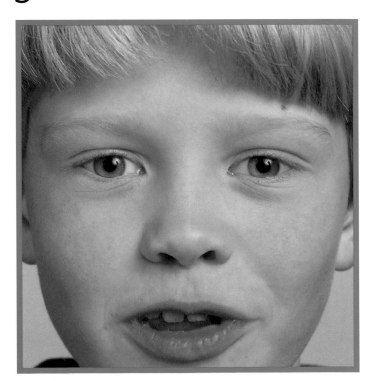

4 We need light to see.

5 Our eyes see colors.

6 Our eyes tell us if something is big, small, near, or far.

7 Seeing helps to keep us safe.

8 Glasses help people to see more clearly.

9 Blind people see very badly or not at all.

10 We must look after our eyes.

Index

About this book

I Know That! is designed to introduce children to the process of gathering information and using reference books, one of the key skills needed to begin more formal learning at school. For this reason, each book's structure reflects the information books children will use later in their learning career—with key information in the main text and additional facts and ideas in the captions. The panels give an opportunity for further activities, ideas, or discussions. The contents page and index are helpful reference guides.

The language is carefully chosen to be accessible to children just beginning to read. Illustrations support the text but also give information in their own right; active consideration and discussion of images is another key referencing skill. The main aim of the series is to build confidence—showing children how much they already know and giving them the ability to gather new information for themselves. With this in mind, the *I know that...* section at the end of the book is a simple way for children to revisit what they already know as well as what they have learned from reading the book.